About the Author

Samia Bazzi has worked as a professional translator for over 15 years and for the past 13 years has been involved in teaching translation and different branches of linguistics at the Lebanese University. She has published extensively on language, culture, and ideology. Her book Arab News and Conflict: A Multidisciplinary Discourse Study has been used as a reference in leading universities in the world on the relationship between language and politics.

Samia Bazzi

TASTE THE ARABIC PROVERBS

Copyright © Samia Bazzi (2017)

The right of Samia Bazzi to be identified as author of this work has been asserted by her in accordance with section 77 and 78 of the Copyright, Designs and Patents Act 1988.

All rights reserved. No part of this publication may be reproduced, stored in a retrieval system, or transmitted in any form or by any means, electronic, mechanical, photocopying, recording, or otherwise, without the prior permission of the publishers.

Any person who commits any unauthorized act in relation to this publication may be liable to criminal prosecution and civil claims for damages.

A CIP catalogue record for this title is available from the British Library.

ISBN 9781786934512 (Paperback)
ISBN 9781786934529 (Hardback)
ISBN 9781786934536 (eBook)

www.austinmacauley.com

First Published (2017)
Austin Macauley Publishers Ltd.
25 Canada Square
Canary Wharf
London
E14 5LQ

TABLE OF CONTENTS

Introduction	9
Parents And Children	13
Failure And Success	14
Trust And Distrust	17
Fools And Wise Men	19
Greed And Hunger	26
Evil Doings	28
Poverty, Luxury, And Festivities	29
Naivety And Knowingness	33
Conflicts And Confrontations	36
Religious	41
Gratitude And Ingratitude	45
The Bad Guest	47
Patience And Procrastination	49
Power, Bribery, And Corruption	52
Scandal	55
Us And Them	56
Weather And Seasons	60
Good And Bad Luck	63
Entertaining And Hospitality	66
Destiny	69
Love And Marriage	70
Liars And Cheats	73
Hopelessness	74
Laziness	76
Spendthrifts And Savers	78
Pretensions And Snobbery	79
Water	82
Respect And Disrespect	83
Usefulness And Handiness	84
The Market	85
Embarrasment And Regret	86
The Drunkards	88
Health	89

Introduction
Defining the Meaning of Proverbs by Proverbs

Proverbs are the adornment of speech.
الأمْثالُ زِينَةُ الكَلام
Proverbs are the wisdom of the generations.
الأمْثالُ حِكْمَةُ الأجيال
Nothing travels so much as a proverb.
أَسْيَرَ مِن مَثل
Popular proverbs are salt to speech.
أمْثالُ العَوام مِلْحُ الكَلام
A proverb never told a lie.
المَثل ما قالْ شِي كذب

A proverb springs from real life. It expresses the truth that a nation realizes, not through theorizing, but through a long, lived experience, in order to advise, reflect upon an event by analogy, or to warn. Proverbs are the images of a nation's life and moralities, its people's disposition, character, and culture. Proverbs are usually sayings that become popular by reflecting and expressing a nation's experience, stories, and history in a short, rhyming form, with a strong rhetorical effect. Proverbs are easily inherited, for they are imprinted in people's memories and circulated to the next generations. Although they may sound backward or archaic, proverbs give savour to the speech of the modern speaker and add originality to our speech.

Anis Freyhe, a famous Lebanese writer who wrote extensively on proverbs, says that "*Mathal* (proverb) is from a common Semitic root signifying simile or comparison… the larger portion of proverbs contain statements of facts based on everyday experience, or metaphors drawn from daily life, or observations of nature and its working. Fondness for parallelism, similes, metaphors, allusions to incongruencies is a common trait which appears in all primitive cultures. This is best illustrated in Jewish and Arabic literature" (Freyhe 1974: 1X-X1).

Some Arabic proverbs date back to the Bible, the Quran, and old Phoenician proverbs. Others originated around historic incidents, based on anecdotes, or answers to riddles to instruct, pass judgment, appeal to human nature, to express sarcasm, to settle disputes, or to solve a vexing problem. Because a proverb lives in a nation's memory, it is easy to use it in common discourse as they express everyday experience in concise cleverly worded aphorisms and eventually become part of national heritage. Many of the proverbs in this book are inspired by rural life in the village. It is interesting to see how people in the city use these sayings and proverbs in their daily discourses to express their feelings and experiences, without knowing the original story behind the proverb. The story becomes forgotten, but the proverb remains in the memory of each generation.

Salaam El-Rasi (1995), another famous Lebanese writer about proverbs, notes that sayings need four reasons to become proverbs. They should: embody the correct analogy, command a consensus in a society, be cognitively comprehensible, and be suitable for the hearer in expressing a real situation.

This book offers a collection of some Arabic proverbs and sayings, with special reference to those from Lebanon. I have collected these proverbs from old people whom I personally know in Lebanon, different books on proverbs (see references), the media, and the daily discourse of ordinary people. The focus is on proverbs and popular sayings related to food and drink, growing and harvesting food, plants, and metaphors concerning eating and health. This shows the place of food in Arab society. It is interesting to see how much more the culture expresses itself through food compared to English-speaking culture. It would also enable me to put international readers in the picture about the main foods mentioned (olive oil/ lentils/ grapes/ honey, etc...) and their place in society as symbols of wealth or poverty and as essentials in the way of life and economy. I hope that through this book, the reader will have a *taste* of some of the Arabic sayings and popular wisdom. The proverbs will also give the foreign reader an idea about the kind of food eaten in the Levant and its role in the lives and cultures of the local people in the region. I have tried to translate each proverb very faithfully in the beginning (in bold), before giving its pragmatic meaning or corresponding proverb or saying in English, if possible. Unfortunately, during translation, the proverb inevitably loses its rhythmic style, and alliteration, but the wisdom behind it can still be understood. Some of the proverbs are classical and some are colloquial. The colloquial ones are attributed to a specific nation, e.g. Lebanese nation; thus, showing their originality by relating such sayings to the Lebanese accent, moralities, and culture. Some proverbs do not need further explanation after direct translation as they are so universal they can be understood without further interpretation.

The proverbs are organized into sub-themes, e.g. family; seasons; hunger; greed; health. The square brackets are used to illustrate the implicit linguistic meanings which are embedded in Arabic through a pronoun or a grammatical feature. The proverbs and sayings under each theme are displayed in alphabetical order in Arabic.

Finally, I am indebted to Ms. Jenifer Spencer, from Heriot-Watt University, UK, for her critical editing of my work and for suggesting some of the equivalent proverbs and sayings in English. I am also grateful to Issam Hourani, Professor of Arabic literature at Notre Dame University, Lebanon, for providing me with further explication of many of the proverbs cited in this book. Furthermore, I am thankful to Randa Challita, Professor of Psychology at the Lebanese University, who inspired me with the general idea of this book.

The Proverbs

PARENTS AND CHILDREN

الآباء يأكلون الحُصْرُم والأبْناء يَضرسون

The parents eat sour [unripe] grapes and the children's teeth are set on edge.

This is said of children who bear the consequences of their parents' wrong doings.

أبُوه بَصل وأُمُّه ثُوم، ومْنَين بَدّها تِجي رِيحْةِ الطَّيِّبة؟

His father is an onion and his mother is garlic; [so] where will good fragrance come from?

When the parents have a bad reputation, the children are bound to suffer the same fate.

إلِّي أمُّه بالبيت ما بيحسّ بالجوع

He whose mother is at home is never hungry.

In the Middle East, the mother's role is very essential in that she keeps the family together, prepares meals for every member, and gives moral support when they are in need of help.

بدْهُن فَتّ خُبز

They need their bread broken.

It is a tradition to crumble bread for the children as they cannot handle the loaf by themselves. This means that you need to work hard to support and provide for the children, hence a lot of bread giving.

FAILURE AND SUCCESS

آخر الطَّحْن قَرْقَعة

The millstones rumble after the wheat is ground.

Said in a situation which ends with failure, especially after long arguments. The image is taken from a millstone which is turning with a rattling noise but grinding no flour.

إلِّي ما بِذوق المُر ما بْيعرف طَعْمِة الحِلُو

He who tastes not the bitter, does not appreciate the taste of the sweet.

Life is made up of both good and bitter experiences. To enjoy the good you should experience the bitter.

إلِّي ما بْيِشرب مِن كَفُّه ما بْيِرْتِوِي

He who does not drink from his own palm does not quench his thirst.

In the countryside, people used to drink from a spring by cupping their hands. The proverb says we should depend on ourselves rather than others to get a job done properly.

بطّيخْتين بفَرد ايد ما بِينحِملوا

Two watermelons in one hand cannot be carried.

Prioritize your work and don't attempt the impossible. As one cannot carry two watermelons in one hand, do not do two or more jobs at the same time. This leads to a delay in your work or you might end up with bad results.

حَلاوة بلا نار ما بِتْكون

There could be no Halawi without fire.

Halawi or Halva is a crystallized paste of sesame seeds (tahini) and sugar. This means it is difficult to achieve something important without adverse effects elsewhere.

cf. You can't make an omelet without breaking eggs.

سَلْق بَيْض

Egg boiling.

Said about easy and quick matters. Also, said when you forbid someone from doing a job hastily. You would say: This isn't egg boiling.

قد ما بِتحُط بالقِدْرة بِتشيل بالمَرْغَفة

As much as you put in the pot you take out with the ladle.

This means that we reap the results of our actions; hence, we must put up with these results. This is also said to mean we should not expect to get good results if our effort was minimal. Another meaning is that any return is proportionate with the investment.

cf. You reap what you sow/ You will only get out of it what you put into it.

كل مين إلو تِم بياكُل

Whoever has a mouth can eat.

Eating is dealing with a situation or earning money. This is said to encourage the helpless to work and earn their living or to make more money.

cf. Get off your backside.

لَوْ الله بْيِسْتِجِيب دُعا الكلاب كانت الدّنْيا بِتْشَنِّي عْظام

If God were to answer dogs' prayers, it would rain bones.

Meaning if we could achieve our goals by merely wishing, life would be very easy.

cf. If 'ifs' and 'ands' were pots and pans/If wishes were horses, beggars would ride.

TRUST AND DISTRUST

آه مِنَك يا بَصلة: مَع كل عَضَّة دَمْعة

Oh, you onion: with every bite [there is] a tear.

This is said of someone who lets you down after a second chance. This reminds us of an onion, for it always makes you cry.

إلْها تِم ياكُل ما لْها تِم يِحْكي

She has a mouth which eats, but not a mouth which speaks.

Said of a girl who is quiet and avoids gossip.

بْيَعمَل من الزّبيبة خَمَّارة

He makes a wine cellar from one raisin.

Said of someone who makes a major issue out of a minor one.

لا تاكُل عَيْش المَنَّان وْلا تِدخُل بيت الظَّنَّان

Eat not the bread of him who reminds you of it, nor enter the house of him who is distrustful.

Admonition to avoid getting help from someone who keeps reminding you he did you a favour in order to pay him in return. It also forbids you from visiting someone who is suspicious of his visitors.

ما بتِنْتقع الحُمَّصة تَحْت لسانُه
The chickpea doesn't soak under his tongue.

Chickpeas are usually soaked in water before boiling to make hummus. Said when someone cannot keep a secret.

FOOLS AND WISE MEN

إجعَلْني بَيْن الأقْدام، ولا تجْعلني بَين الأفْواه

Put me underfoot, but not in the mouths of men.

This is a prayer to God to save one from gossip or metaphorically "big mouths". It expresses the cruelty we feel when people speak ill of us and our dignity. One would rather suffer physically but not morally, for being trodden over can give a temporary pain, but being slandered is limitlessly painful.

إذا كان حَبيبك عسَل لا تلْحَسُه كلّه

If your beloved is honey, don't eat it all.

Do not take advantage of people who are very kind and nice to you.

cf. Don't kill the goose that lays the golden egg.

أعطِ خُبزك للخَبَّاز، ولو أكَل نصْفُه

Give your dough to a baker, even though he may eat half of it.

Give your dough to the baker to bake, even if he uses some of it for himself, or even if you lose some of your money. In other words, refer to specialists and professionals who might overcharge you, but they will still give you better results.

This is said because one might ask less competent people to do a particular job in order to save money; thus, ending in regret.

أكل البَصل بداري أحسَن من أكُل اللّحم عند جاري

Eating onions at my house is better than eating meat at my neighbour's house.

Advice to abstain from degrading oneself.

إلِّي سناتُه طَريّة ما بيكسِّر عليها جوز

He who has soft teeth should not break walnuts.

Advice to be wise and prudent.

cf. People who live in glass houses should not throw stones.

بِبَطْن السّبْع وْلا بِبَطْن الضّبع

May it be in the stomach of the lion rather than in the stomach of a hyena.

If something is to be lost, better to have it taken by someone who has esteem, than someone who is insignificant. The image could be taken from the fact that a lion would only eat a fresh prey; whereas the hyena can feed on rotten prey.

بَدَّك تاكُل عِنَب يمَّا تِقْتُل النّاطور؟

Do you want to eat grapes, or kill the watchman?

A very common proverb said when someone is being unrealistic and impractical. The person might focus on issues that are not related to the direct goal. Eating the grapes is metaphorical for the target. The means to it does not necessarily require "killing the watchman"; any other means could do just as well, as long the goal is reached. Briefly, if you need to attain your goal, you should avoid trouble or violence.

It is also said to mean you should not resort to illegal means if you are capable of procuring things in a harmless way.

بَس تحَمّصْها لا تِحُرقْها

When you roast it, don't burn it.

Roasting is good, but when you overdo something, you might ruin it all. Pay attention to this thin line.

بِسلّي الْحمَى بِقِشْر البَطّيخ

He distracts fever with watermelon peels.

This is said ironically of someone who pretends to fix a serious situation by doing nothing. It is also said ironically of remedies which give only temporary relief. The rind of a watermelon is placed on the forehead of someone who has a fever, but the relief is temporary.

بِمَلّي بالسَّلّة

He carries water in a basket!
Said of a fool.

بْيِشْرَب البَحْر وْيِغْصّ بِالسّاقِية

He drinks the sea, but chokes on the rivulet.

Said of people who do great works, but stop at trivial matters. It is also said of those who spend a lot of money, but hold back when they have to spend a bit more for something they need. It is also said of thinkers who do not complete their work when it is about to be done.

جَوّعْ هِرَّك ياكُل فارَكْ، شَبّع كَلْبَك يِحْرُسْ دارك

Keep your cat hungry and it will eat up your mice; keep your dog full and it will guard your house.

ذَيْنْتَك مِش بْعيدِة عَن تِمَّك
Your ear is not far from your mouth.

This means you had better say this thing to yourself rather than telling others.

السُّنْبِلة العَالية فارِغة
An ear of wheat standing high is empty.

This is said of haughty, empty-headed, and useless people, who are like tall wheat spikes. Such people fool others with their false appearances, whereas, modest people are like a full spike bending down before harvesting.

العْنْقود العَالي حُصْرُم
The high grape clusters are sour.

We tend to mention the bad qualities of something we fail to attain, in order to save face, just as the fox in the ancient Greek fables of Aesop said *the high grapes were unripe and sour*. This means do not fool yourself.

cf. Sour grapes!

قالوا لُه، لَيْش عَم تِنفُخ في اللَّبن؟ قال كاوينِي حَليب
They asked him: Why are you blowing into this yogurt?

He answered: I was scalded by the milk.

Or, he who complains about yogurt is he who was scalded by it while it was still hot milk. Yogurt is made out of hot milk. When it settles and cools down, a small portion of yogurt is added to this milk and it subsequently turns into yogurt. Hence, one does not need to blow into the finished yoghurt to reduce the heat. This is said about a person who is always very cautious due to a bad incident experienced in the past.

cf. A burnt child dreads the fire/ Once bitten, twice shy.

قُل لُّه ثَوْر، بِقُول لَّك احلِبُه
Tell him, "It's an ox," he says, "Milk it."
Said of a stupid person who, after being told how to deal with things on a number of occasions, continues to ask the same question or prove his stupidity.

كِثرِتِ الطَّبَّاخين شَوْشَطِ الطَّعام
Too many cooks burn the food.
Meaning when many people are in charge of the same thing at the same time, it ends up in chaos.
cf. Too many cooks spoil the broth.

لا تقول فول حتَّى تُحُطَّ بالمَكْيول
Do not say I have beans until you measure them in the scale.
Do not say you have gained something until you know who will buy them and how much they will pay. This very common proverb is also used in other situations including the political, meaning do not say you reached your goals till you have dealt with them in reality.
cf. Don't count your chickens before they hatch.

ما بِقَرْقِع بالدَّست إلاَّ العُظام
It is only the bones which rattle in the pot.
The bones usually make a rattling noise when boiling, but the meat doesn't. This means trivial people or mobs make noise and cause fuss, unlike the wise who keep silent.
cf. Empty vessels make the most noise.

ما بيعرِف طَعمِة تِمُه

He does not know the taste of his own mouth.

He is ill-mannered; a man of no taste.

مِثل البَقرة الّي بْتِحْلُب وْبِتْكِب حَليبْها

Like a cow which gives milk but then spills it.

Said of someone who is usually giving, but wastes important chances in life because of wrong decisions.

مِثل القَرْع، كِلّما كِبِر بِخِفّ

Like a gourd, the older it gets, the lighter it gets.

Said of an old man who in addition to losing his hair, becomes senile.

cf. He's losing his marbles.

مثل يَلّلي يطغمي زَلابيه للكَلب

Like offering *Zalabieh* to a dog.

Zalabieh is a tasty dessert made of flour and sugar usually offered to refined people. This means don't give valuable things to people who won't appreciate them.

cf. Don't cast pearls before swine (from the Bible).

شو بِعَرِّف الحَمير بْأَكِل الزَّنْجَبِيل؟

What do donkeys know about the taste of ginger?

Do not give valuable things to those who don't appreciate them. Also said to a man who has never tried any delicacies, but nevertheless ridicules people who develop a taste for them.

مِن فاتُه اللَّحم بِشْبَع من المَرق

He, who missed the meat, can eat its broth.

A little bit is better than nothing! This is said to ease disappointment. Also, an advice warning one not to miss both but at least to get the substitute.

مِن وَفَّر غَداه لَعَشاه ما شِمْتِت فيه عِداه

He who saves his lunch for his supper, his enemies won't gloat over it.

Advice to be wise and reasonable.

الوِعاء الكُبير بِساغ الصّغير

The large vessel contains the smaller vessel.

An admonition for forgiveness. As big vessels can assimilate the smaller ones, so a wise person can ignore or forgive the follies of those who are smaller-minded or less worthy than him. They can be smaller by age, position, or any social status. The proverb also means people who have more should help those who have less.

GREED AND HUNGER

أَكل البيْضة والتَّقْشيرة

He ate the egg and its shell too.
An expression when everything has been consumed in a greedy manner.

أَكل أَصابِعُه

He ate his own fingers.
This is said about someone who liked the food so much to the point that he was about to eat his own fingers. In the olden days, people used to eat using their fingers.

الجُوع بْيرمي عَ الهلاك

Hunger makes one throw oneself to death.
A hungry man is prepared to do anything just to eat, such as stealing or any other wrong and violent acts.

الجوع كافِر

Hunger is an infidel.
It means when man is desperate for food, there is little patience, less forgiveness, and bad temper.
cf. A hungry man is an angry man.

شو أَحْلى مْنِ العَسل؟ خَلّ بَلاش

What is sweeter than honey? Free vinegar.

Usually said by stingy people, who would find pleasure in getting low-quality things if they were for free.

عِند الغَدا ما حَدا لحَدا

At lunch everyone is left alone.

Lunch is the main meal in the Middle East. So, when stomachs are busy, minds are absent.

قالوا للجُوعان: ثْنَيْن و ثْنَيْن؟ قال أَرْبَعة أَرْغِفة

They asked a hungry man, "two plus two?" He answered, "Four loaves".

ما بِقيمَك عَن غداك إلاَّ أكبر أَعْداك

Nobody but your worst enemy would make you leave your dinner.

Advice not to visit at meal-times.

EVIL DOINGS

إتَّفَقوا الفِيران عَلى خُبز الجيران

The mice have agreed to eat up the neighbour's bread.

Said of wicked people who plan evil doings.

ذَوَّقُه زوم الزَّيتون

He made him taste the marinating water of olives.

Usually olives are soaked in water before they become edible and this kind of water has a very bitter taste. This expression is said of people who made you suffer to a large extent.

POVERTY, LUXURY, AND FESTIVITIES

إذا كانَت العائلة بِحاجَة للزَّيت، يُحرّم تَقديمُه للجَامِع

If a family is in need of oil, it is forbidden to donate it to the mosque.

A person must fulfill his family's needs before making a donation, even if the donation was meant to be given to holy places. Olive oil is a basic necessity in an Arab household.

إن حِضِر القَمح والزَّيْت تْسَوكَرِت مُونْة البَيْت

When wheat and oil are provided, then the family's provisions are ensured.

This proverb refers to farmers in Lebanon who buy winter provisions in autumn. Wheat and oil are the most important items and once these are stored, the farmer feels secure.

cf. Make hay while the sun shines/ Save for a rainy day.

الله طَعَم كُولْ واطْعِم

God fed you, so eat and then feed.

God has bestowed his grace upon you; so eat, and give others to eat. This is specifically said to the rich, who should be giving to others.

إلِّي ما بِيرْبى عَ سُفْرِة أَبوه ما بْيِشْبَع

He who is not raised at his father's dining table will never be full.

Those who have not seen what is good during childhood will never be satisfied. This also refers to the hard life which orphans often experience.

راح الفَلّاح عالسُوق، ما اشْتَرى غير خبز مَرْقوق

The farmer went to the market, the only thing he bought was marquq bread.

Marquq is traditional homemade bread which farmers usually eat. The market refers to city shops which are full of many other choices. However, simple people or peasants cannot buy what people in the city buy; they usually end up buying what they use in the village. This proverb means that people are influenced by their own environment and background.

نِزْل الفَلّاح لِلْمْدينِة ما اسْتَحْلى غَيْرِ الدِّبْس بِطْحينِة

A peasant came down to the city. The only thing he fancied to eat was molasses mixed with sesame oil.

A similar proverb with a similar meaning. Molasses mixed with sesame oil is usually the only dessert the peasant has at home.

صايِرْلَك مِن يِطْبُخ لك وليش حَتَّى تُحَرْوِق صابيعَك؟

You have someone to cook for you, why burn your fingers?

This is said to a woman to rest if she has a servant or a family member to help her; or to someone who does not need to labour if he has someone else to do the job.

العِز لِلرِّز والبُرغُل شَنَق حَالُه

Honour to rice; let burghul hang itself!

Rice in the olden days was a delicacy, but burghul (wheat that has been steamed or parboiled, dried and ground) used to be the staple food of farmers and poorer classes. The proverb means new modern things nowadays have made the good old things disappear.

كُول خِبْزِة وْتينِة وبَرْطِع بالمْدينِة وْلا تاكُل لَحْمِة سْمينِة وتْبات عَلَيْها حَزينِة

Eat a piece of bread and a fig and frolic about in the city, rather than eat fat meats and go to bed in sorrow.

It is better to live a poor life in a city than living a rich life in a village, where life is boring.

ما بِبكي عَ رَمضان، بِبكي عَ أكْلاتِه

I do not cry over Ramadan, I cry over its dishes.

During the holy month of Ramadan, Muslims fast and celebrate their fast-breaking by eating elaborate meals with their families and friends. This is said when someone puts emphasis on the gatherings or feasts rather than on the spiritual value of fasting.

مِن أكَل خِبْز بِالدَّيْن ارْحَموه، وْمِن أكَل لَحْم بِالدَّيْن ارجُموه

He who borrows money to eat bread, pity him; but he who borrows money to eat meat, stone him.

Meaning a person who borrows money to spend it on necessities deserves mercy, but someone who borrows money to spend it on unnecessary things deserves no mercy. The word *stone* in Arabic is used for rhyming and alliteration.

ناس بِصوموا، ناس بِعوموا

Some people fast, some people float.

Some people are destitute; whereas others enjoy affluence.

يَوْم كان بْكَرْمِي دِبْس يا كِثْرة أَحْبابي، وْيَوم صار كَرْمي بِيْسْ يا قِلّة أصحابي

When I had molasses [grapes] in my vineyard how many loving people I had; when my vineyard became dry, how scarce my friends have become!

This is inspired by rural life in Lebanon, where people come to lush vineyards and leave the dry ones. In the same way, people flock to those who have money and wealth. It is said of opportunists who would just leave you if they couldn't benefit from you.

NAIVETY AND KNOWINGNESS

إرميه بالبَحر بْيِطْلَع وبْتِمُّه سَمَكِة

Throw him into the sea, he comes up with a fish in his mouth.

Said of a clever person who avails himself of a misfortune.

cf. He comes up smelling of roses.

باتِتْ جوعانة وْجَوْزْها خبّاز

She went to bed hungry, though her husband is a baker.

This is said about those who don't know how to benefit from what they have either because of laziness or lack of intelligence.

بَعدُه الحَليب عَ تِمُّه

Milk is still on his mouth.

Said mockingly of an adult who always behaves like a child.

بِغَمِّس بَرَّاتْ الصَّحْن

He dips outside the plate.

Referring to the traditional Mediterranean practice of dipping one's bread in olive oil. Said of someone who lost track, or gone astray.

بيِلْحَس الدِّبس عَن الطَّحينة
He licks the molasses off the tahini.

In the Middle East, people eat molasses (made of grapes or carob as an alternative to sugar). Molasses is sometimes mixed with tahini (sesame paste). It is usually impossible to separate them once mixed. The proverb refers to a clever person who, metaphorically speaking, is capable of separating molasses from tahini. This is often said of a crafty person who can do hard jobs.

الدّيك الفَصيح مِن داخِل البَيْضة بِصيح
The eloquent cock crows while inside the egg.

This is said of talents that start from childhood or at a very early age. The expression is inspired by village life and its tendency to exaggeration tells us that the clever cock starts crowing from the egg before it even hatches.

طِلِع زامِط مِثل الشَّعرة من العَجين
He came out clean like a hair out of the dough.

Said of people who do mean or illegal things but always manage to seem innocent.

cf. He/she always comes up smelling of roses.

طِلِع طُلوع الكوسَى ونِزِل نَزِلة الباذِنْجان
He ascended like courgettes and descended like eggplants.

Usually courgettes grow upwards and eggplants downwards. This is said of someone who reaches a high position without merit but soon falls to the bottom.

مِسكين وْوَقَّع بْسَل تين

A poor man falling upon a basket full of figs.

Said of an inexperienced or deprived person who does not know how to handle a serious or sensitive situation; hence, stuck in a pitiable way.

CONFLICTS AND CONFRONTATIONS

إِشْغِل الكَلْب بْعَظْمِة

Occupy the dog by throwing it a bone.

Do not let materialistic antagonists, who make a loud noise, bother you. Treat them as you would treat a noisy dog who gets distracted with a bone. This is also said in political discourse.

إِلِّي بِخَزِّق خِبِز النَّاس، النَّاس بِتْخَزِّق خِبزُه

He who tears people's loaves, people will tear his loaves.

Don't ill-treat others or you will be ill-treated.
cf. Do as you would be done by.

إِلِّي بِغَرِبِل النَّاسْ، النَّاسْ بْينخْلُوه

He who sifts people with a coarse sieve shall find people sifting him with a fine sieve.

If one finds faults in others, he should be prepared to be a subject to closer scrutiny.

إِلِّي بِيَعرِف بْيَعرِف وإِلِّي ما بْيعرِف بِقول كَف عَدَس

He who knows, knows, and he who does not know would say 'a handful of lentils'.

This is said when serious matters are taken lightly. This refers to a story: a few farmers had a quarrel in a field where they grew lentils. The reason for the quarrel was that one of them had been flirting with one of the female workers. He was confronted by another farmer, and made off whilst carrying a handful of lentils. The people who gathered to separate the quarreling farmers thought the quarrel was about this handful of lentils which he was carrying while attempting to flee. His pursuer said the above quote which became a Lebanese proverb.

ما هي عَلى الرُّمَّانِة، القُلُوب مَلْيانِة

It was not because of the pomegranate, it was because the hearts were full.

Two children fought over a pomegranate. This caused a fight among their parents and then among the two factions the parents represented. So, the conflict was not really because of the pomegranate.

إلِّي ما بيِعْجْبُه يِشْرَب البَحْر

He who does not like it let him go and drink up the sea.

An expression said in a confrontational tone meaning "So what are you going to do about it?"

cf. Like it or lump it.

بَطِّيخ يْكَسِّر بَعْضُه

Let the watermelons break against one another.

It is harmless as long as it is watermelons breaking against each other. Said when there are people causing trouble and you shouldn't interfere. Let them do what they like and hurt each other.

بِلُّوها واشْرَبوا مَيِّتْها

Soak it and drink its water.

This refers to soaking paper that could be a certificate for example. It is said mockingly to those who carry university certificates and find no jobs. So, better soak the paper and drink its water as this paper has become useless.

This is also said mockingly when you don't care for what other people or parties decide officially against you. Some politicians in Lebanon use this expression against opponents in situations where there are penalties imposed against them. For instance, the leader of Hezbollah, a militia group in Lebanon, addressed the EU once by saying: "*Soak your terror list and drink its water.*"

تْعَشَّاه قَبْل ما بِتْغَدَّاه

He supped him before the other fellow lunched him.

It is better to take action to forestall someone who is likely to be planning something against you.

شُو أَحْلى مِنِ الْحَلاوِة؟ صُلْح بَعْد عَداوِة

What is sweeter than Halawi? Reconciliation after enmity.

Halawi is crystallized paste of sesame seeds (Tahini) and sugar.

طابِخِ السَّمّ آكْلُه

He who cooks poison, poison shall he eat.

كُول كُرْه واشرَب كُرْه ولا تُعاشِر كُرْه

Let your food be detestable, and your drink abominable, but do not associate with an abominable person.

لا مُصالحَة بِلا مُمالحَة

No reconciliation without sharing food.

Sharing food in the Middle East is symbolic of good relationships with family, neighbours, or friends. This is advice to celebrate or share food after reconciliation.

مِفْتاح البطن لقْمِة، ومِفْتاح الشَّر كلِمة

The key to your stomach is one mouthful, and the key to a quarrel is one word.

This means when you start one thing, you continue doing it whether it is good or bad. Just as the first mouthful is the key to your appetite; so the first word is the key to a quarrel. The proverb warns against hasty words which lead to fighting.

وحدها الشَّجرة المُثمِرة تُرجم بالحجارة

Only the fruitful tree gets stoned.

Taken from the image of a tree laden with fruit. This is used in situations where one would refer to a very productive and good person who gets attacked or receives destructive criticism.

وِصِل السِّكين لِلْعَظْم

The knife has cut deep to the bone.

Said when a situation has reached its limit.

cf. Enough is enough/ It was the last straw that broke the camel's back/ That's the last straw.

يا ربّي تْشَرْدِقْني بْريقي تَ أَعْرِف عَدُوّي مِن صديقي

Oh God, may I choke on my own saliva, to know who is my enemy or my friend.

Based on a superstition that when one chokes in swallowing, and happens to be thinking of another person at the same time, or when someone's name is mentioned, then this person must be an enemy.

يْضُرِّ المِعْدِة وْلا بِنْفَع الإعدا

Rather let it hurt your stomach than give it away to enemies.

Rather that it hurts than letting your enemy avail of it is advice to refrain from helping your enemy even if you have to suffer.

RELIGIOUS

أَعطِنا خُبزَنا كَفافَ يَوْمِنا

Give us this day our daily bread.

Based on a biblical prayer to remind one that we rely on God as our provider to meet our materialistic and spiritual needs.

أَنتُم مِلْحُ الأَرْض، فَإِذا فَسد المِلْح فَبِماذا يُمَلَّح؟

Ye are the salt of the earth: but if the salt have lost his savour, wherewith shall it be salted?

Ye are the salt of the earth: but if the salt have lost his savour, wherewith shall it be salted? It is thenceforth good for nothing, but to be cast out, and to be trodden under foot of men.

Matthew, 5:13

This proverb is taken from the Bible and is commonly used by the Christian community in Lebanon to call for peace amongst the divided sects in this war-torn country. As salt preserves food from corruption, so do the disciples of the Messiah have to preserve the world from general corruption and calamities.

احذروا صَوْلَةَ الكريم اذا جاعَ، واللَّئيم إذا شَبِعَ

Fear the attack of a noble person when he is hungry, and that of an ignoble person when he is full.

An Islamic proverb meaning that a man of prestige and esteem never tolerates humiliation or disgrace. If his honour is assailed, he will leap like a hungry lion.

However, an ignoble person who is raised beyond his rank will assail another man's position to make up for what he had previously lacked. In other words, richness is ugly in the hands of the vile, as ugly as it is when a generous man is hungry. The proverb advises one not to let a sudden change in fortunes affect us negatively.

cf. He's got a chip on his shoulder.

اخْذَر اللَّئيم اذا شَبِع والكَريم إذا جاع

Beware of the ignoble when full, and the generous when hungry.

This is a similar proverb, but in its colloquial Arabic form.

اطْلبوا الخَير مِن بُطون شَبِعت، ثُمَ جاعَت لأنَّ الخَير باقٍ فِيها، ولا تَطلبوا الخَيْر مِن بُطون جاعَت ثُمَ شَبِعَت، لأنَّ الشُّحَ باقَ فِيها

Ask for good things from stomachs that were full then became hungry, because the good is still inside them, but don't ask for good things from stomachs that were hungry then became full, because stinginess is still inside them.

This is an Islamic proverb which means when someone has lived an honorable life, this will always be part of his character. "Full" does not necessarily refer to money, but to satisfactoriness and virtuousness. Such people will always be giving. However; those, who have always lived hungry for what others possess, are unlikely to help, as they are not used to giving.

This is also said in situations where we should not expect any good from those who have suddenly become rich, as they will always be greedy.

أيُحِبُّ أَحَدُكُم أَن يَأْكُلَ لَحْمَ أَخِيهِ مَيِّتاً؟

Would any of you like to eat the flesh of his dead brother?

The Holy Quran, Al-Hujurat, 12

A Quranic proverb meaning no one would even like to think of such an abomination as eating the flesh of his brother. But when the brother is dead, and the flesh is carrion, abomination is added to abomination. In the same way, we are asked to refrain from gossip and backbiting. It is a sin added to sin when we do injustice to innocent men and women, and say false things about them when they are absent.

تُعرف الشَّجرة بِثَمَرها

A tree is known by its fruit.

Man is judged by his achievements.

No good tree bears bad fruit, nor does a bad tree bear good fruit.

Luke 6:43

لا نَأكل من هذا الخُبز

We don't eat this bread.

We don't get involved in illegal means of earning. This is based on:

For they eat the bread of wickedness, and drink the wine of violence.

Proverbs: 4:17

لاينبغي للعَبدِ أَن يَثِقَ بِخَصلتين: العافِية والغِنى. بَيْناً تراهُ مُعافىً إذْ سَقِمَ، وَبَيْناً تَراهُ غَنِياً إذْ افْتَقَرَ

There are two good things a man shouldn't trust: health and wealth, because many a healthy man soon falls sick and many a wealthy man soon falls destitute.

An Islamic proverb.

لَقْمَتُة مُغَمَّسِة بِالدَّم

His bread is dipped in blood.

This means that someone has toiled with dignity in order to earn his own livelihood. During the journey of toil, one might face dangers and threats; thus this bite of bread is said to be dipped with his blood. This saying is influenced by religious discourses amongst the Christian communities in the Middle East:

For my flesh is true food, and my blood is true drink.
John: 6:55

مَنْهومان لا يشْبَعان: طالِبُ عِلْم وطالِبُ دُنْيا

Two greedy persons never get full: the seeker of knowledge and the seeker of this world.

An Islamic proverb meaning two different types of people never get satiated: the scientists who seek knowledge, and those who seek world's materialistic pleasures.

GRATITUDE AND INGRATITUDE

أَكَلني لَحماً ورَماني عَظْماً
He had me as meat and threw me away as bones.

Said of opportunists who sponge on you and take advantage of you. Such people would turn away when they can no longer benefit from you.

بْتِشْرَب مْن البير وبْتِرْمي فيه حَجَر؟
Do you drink from a well and cast a stone into it?

The question means "do not cast a stone into the well from which you drink". In other words, do not meet goodness with denial and ingratitude. This is similar to throwing stones and polluting the clear water from which you have just drunk.

بسْ شِبِع قال العِنب مُر
After he became full, he said the grapes were bitter.

Said of ungrateful people.

بْياكُلْ خِبْزَكْ وبْيِدْعَسْ عَ كَعْبَك
He eats your bread and steps on your heels.
He causes harm to his benefactor.

البيت اللِّي بْتاكُل مِنّو ما تِدْعي عَلَيْه بِالْخَراب

Do not invoke destruction upon the house from which you eat.

This proverb forbids ingratitude. Do not be ungrateful to those who have been kind to you.

cf. Don't bite the hand that feeds you.

خِبْز الرِّجال: دَيْن على الرِّجال وصَدَقة على الأَنْذال

A noble man's bread: A debt to the honourable; a charity to the wretched.

Bread here is a metaphor for giving to others. This bread will be received by an honourable person with gratitude, as if it is a debt that should be paid back one day, whereas, a vile person or a miser will accept help from others as charity, as he takes but doesn't give.

طعْمَيتُه عَسَل، عَضّ أصبَعي

I fed him honey, he bit my finger.

Said of ungrateful people who harm you after you have been kind to them

cf. Don't bite the hand that feeds you.

وجّ ما بْيِضْحَك لَرْغِيفِ السُّخْن

His face would not smile even at a hot loaf of bread.

Fresh bread brings joy to our hearts and makes us thankful. This mocks sulky people who never seem to be pleased at the nice things in life.

cf. If he smiled, his face would crack.

.

THE BAD GUEST

آكِل، شارِب، نايِم

Given food, drink, and bed.

This is said of opportunists who benefit from others without having to spend their own money. It also refers to demanding guests.

إلِّي معوَّد ع خبزاتَك، كل ما شافك بِجُوع

He who is used to your bread gets hungry every time he sees you.

Said of a scrounger who becomes dependent on someone's favours. Advice to avoid opportunists.

بْكِلّ غُرْس إلُه قُرصْ

He gets a cake at every wedding.

This is said of someone who likes to be involved in every event. It is also said of inquisitive people who like to benefit from every occasion.

cf. He has a finger in every pie.

عايِش على صْحوننا

He lives on our dishes.

Said of a person who sponges on others.

كثرة التَّأهيل تجْلب الضَّيف الثَّقيل

Too much welcoming brings in heavy guests.

Some people are too hospitable and this invites opportunists to sponge on their kindness. The proverb advises one to extend hospitality with discrimination.

cf. A constant guest is never welcome.

PATIENCE AND PROCRASTINATION

إلِّي بدُّه ياكُل عَسَل بْيِصْبُر عَلى قَرْص النَّحْل

He who wants to eat honey should bear the stings of bees.

This is said when one needs to be patient in order to reach good results. A similar saying in Arabic tells us: If one wants to eat the sweets of life, he should be able to bear the bitter parts of it.

cf. Patience is a virtue.

إلِّي بْياكُلْ هَالأَكْلات بَدُّه يْموت هَالْمَوْتات/ بْيوقَع هالوَقْعَات

He who eats such delicacies should die such a death/should be prepared to fall into such pitfalls.

Or more simply, people who want to enjoy the good things should be prepared to put up with their downside/disadvantages.

cf. Take the rough with the smooth.

إلِّي بيصبُر يَاكُل طَيّب

He who is patient eats good food.

Cooking tasty food needs patience. This is advice to be patient to reach good results.

بَصَلْتَك مَحْروقَة

Your onion is burnt.
Usually, onions are fried at a low or moderate temperature and need to be stirred all the time. However, if you are in a hurry you would use a high temperature to try to fry them quickly. The result is usually burnt onions. This is said of impatient people who generally end up with unsatisfactory results.

بِالمِشْمِشْ

In the apricot [season].
Apricots usually take long to grow and ripen, hence one has to wait for another year to eat them again. This expression is said sarcastically when someone postpones a job, puts something off indefinitely, refuses to pay back, or fails to fulfill a promise on time.

بَيْضة اليَوْم ولا دَجاجِة بُكرَة

Better the egg of today than the hen of tomorrow.
This proverb advises one to be realistic by benefiting from the present moment rather than rejecting it, as the egg might not hatch tomorrow.

cf. A bird in the hand is worth two in the bush.

حَبّة حَبّة أَكل العنب

He ate the grapes one by one.
Advice to take matters step by step without hurrying.
cf. One step at a time.

لَو كانت الدّنيا بَيْضة كان الواحد قَشّرها

Had the world been an egg, one would have peeled it.

An egg simply needs peeling. If the world was like an egg, life would be so easy. This is advice to be patient.

مِن صَبَر ع الحُصرُمْ أَكَلُه دِبْس (عِنب)

He who waits for berries shall eat them as molasses [ripe grapes].

Molasses also refers to sweet syrup made of ripe grapes. An admonition for patience.

الوعاء بِساع مَلانُه

A vessel can contain its utmost.

We cannot expect anyone to sacrifice more than he or she can, as there is limit to everyone's patience.

POWER, BRIBERY, AND CORRUPTION

إلِّي بْياكُل خُبز السُّلطان بْيِضْرُب بِسَيْفُه

He who eats the bread of the Sultan is able to strike with the Sultan's sword.

Said of senior officials who are oppressive like their ruler.

البَيْضة ما بْتِكْسُر حَجَر

An egg does not break a stone.
A weak person cannot oppose a very powerful one.

اطعِم الفَم تسْتحي العَين

Feed the mouth, and the eye looks away.
Feed the mouth is metaphorical for giving money. This means when someone gives money away to please certain people, he can hide his bad traits with this money. In other words, bribing people makes them overlook the bad or negative things about the person who bribes them. Hence, with every amount paid, the eye will look away and won't see the faults and follies of the corrupt person. Another meaning is to bribe a judge or a senior official and he will overlook your guilt.

دُودِ الجِبْن مِنُّه وفيه
دُودِ الخَلّ مِنُّه وْفِيه

The worms of cheese are of the cheese itself/ the worms in vinegar are of the vinegar itself.

Said of the bad effect of a corrupted or violent social environment. Like vinegar or cheese, which seem to form worms from within, so the traits of the corrupt or wicked people are the result of their own bad environment.

الزِّيْت ما بيطلَع إلاّ بالمِعْصار

Oil can only be extracted by the press.

The proverb refers to an old traditional way of oil extracting. Some people are like olives, you need to be hard on them to get the good out of them. The proverb means force is sometimes the only means of getting things done.

مِثل الزَّيتون، ما بْيجي إلاّ بالرَّص

Like olives: they sweeten with bruising.

Said when force must be applied to the ruled. This is similar to olives which can only give you a good taste after bruising.

مِثْلِ الجَوْز ما بْيِتّاكل غَيْر كَسْر

Like a walnut, that can't be eaten unless you crack it.

Said when you need to use force to get something from someone.

السَّمَك الكُبير بْياكُل الصّغير

Big fish eat small fish.

Meaning the powerful can do what they like, even if they follow illegal means.

كَلَّفوا القِرْد بْنَغْف الطّحين

They delegated the monkey to sprinkle the flour.

Sprinkling flour requires extra care because it can cause a mess. If a monkey was to do this job, one could imagine the consequences. This is said about entrusting non-professional or unworthy people to carry out big and responsible jobs in society. It is said in Lebanon, particularly when referring to unworthy politicians.

كوُل واشرَب و خَلّي الدَّنيا تخرَب

Eat, drink, and let the world go to ruin.

Meaning just enjoy yourself while you can.

cf. Eat, drink and be merry.

It is also an expression said of people who enjoy themselves while ignoring terrible things that are happening.

cf. Fiddle while Rome burns.

SCANDAL

إلِّي ما بياكُل ثوم ما بِتطْلَع ريحْتُه

He who does not eat garlic does not stink.

Said about wrong acts some try to hide, but are soon discovered.

cf. There's no smoke without a fire.

يا داخِل بَيْن البَصَلِة والثُّومِة، يا شامِمْ ريحَة مَيْشُومِة (يا خَارج بالرِّيحة المَشْومة)

You, who insert yourself between onions and garlic, you will come out with an offensive smell.

Said to stop someone from interfering in some dirty scandal, or from interfering in other peoples' business. Inquisitive people shouldn't be surprised when they come to some harm – it is a natural result of being nosy. Just as it is natural to smell the odours coming from the onion and the garlic.

cf. Curiosity killed the cat.

يا داخِل بَيْن البَصَلِة وقِشْرتها، ما يْنالَك إلاَّ صَنَّتْها

You, who try to get between an onion and its peel, the only thing you get is its stinky smell.

A similar saying with a similar meaning.

US AND THEM

إن كان الكنافة بيذخِلها ثُوم، الموراني بحِبّ الرُوم

If garlic can be added to knafi, a Maronite can love a Greek.

Knafi is a very rich dessert made of semolina, cheese, butter, and sugar syrup.

So it is easier for garlic to be added to this popular Arabic dessert, than it is for a Maronite (Catholic) to love a Greek Orthodox person. This shows the religious divisions in Lebanon.

أهْلَك وْلَو أكلوا اللَّحْم ما بيكسروا العَظْم

Though your kinsmen may eat your flesh, they will not break your bones.

Kinship in the Middle East is a very strong tie. If one of your relatives hurts you, he won't destroy you completely.

cf. Blood is thicker than water.

بياكلوا مِن ذات الصَّحن

They eat from the same plate.

Said of people who share things or have lived together in good and bad times.

cf. They grew up under the same roof.

بَيْنَنا خُبْز وَمِلْح

Between us there is bread and salt.

Said when referring to sharing experiences in the past, whether in good or in bad. This is said as reminder of good old company.

تْعشَّ عِنْد الدّرزي، ونام عِنْد النّصراني

Have supper at a Druze's, but spend the night at a Christian's.

This is a racist proverb which reflects what some Lebanese believe. Some Lebanese believe that the Druzes (a religious sect) are very hospitable, but they cannot be trusted. Such proverbs originated during periods of religious disturbances.

رْغيف بِرْغيف وْلا يْبَات جارَك جُوعان

A loaf of bread for a loaf of bread rather than [seeing] your neighbour sleep hungry.

This proverb emphasizes the importance of good neighbourliness in Arab society. Sharing the very little you have with your neighbour acknowledges the rights of your neighbour.

شْعيرْنا وْلا قَمْح غَيْرْنا

Our own barley rather than the wheat of others.

Barley is considered cheaper than wheat. This proverb encourages people not to choose the foreign, even if the foreign thing is better. It calls for self-sufficiency and pride in all fields, whether at the social level or the economic level. In the social context, it encourages people not to marry out of the community. In the economic context, it encourages using local products.

طَنْجرة وْلِقْيِتْ غَطاها

A pot that has found its lid.

Said sarcastically of a couple who are similar in their traits, or attitude (usually refers to bad traits).

cf. They're two of a kind/ They're birds of a feather!

فإنَّ للشّيءِ أشباهَ تُناط به كالسّمنِ أطيب ما يذكو به العسل
وعند ذي حَسَبٍ تَلقى ذوي نسبٍ ومع "مجدَّرةٍ يُستَمرىءُ البَصل

With honey the best match is margarine, with Mjaddara the best match you find is onions.

People like to eat honey with margarine; but, with Mjaddara (a lentil dish) the best match is onions. In the old days, honey and margarine were the foods of the rich; whereas, lentils were the food of the poor. This is said about matching. With the rich you will find the wealthy; and with the poor you will find the poor.

cf. Birds of a feather flock together.

فولِة وانقسَمِت

A horse bean that has been split in two.

Said jokingly of two people who are very similar.

cf. They are like two peas in a pod.

كُول لَقْمْتي بِتْصير نَقْمْتي

Share my bread and you shall be one of my worries.

Said lightheartedly to those who share you a loaf of bread, e.g. your family. When family members share a loaf, they also share each other's worries.

ما حدا بِنادي عَ زَيْتُه عِكِر

No one calls out: "my oil is rancid".

In the old days, olive oil vendors would call out: "Oil, oil, pure clear oil!" - meaning no one would say bad things about what he owns or what concerns him.

مِن عُظام الرَّقْبة

Of the bones of the neck.

An expression said of close and dear relatives. They can be as close and dear as the bones of your neck.

هالكعِك مِش مِن هالعَجين

This cake cannot be from this dough.

When the cake is baked, it holds the characteristics of the dough from which it was made. This is said of someone who looks different from others in his own group because he has different traits.

WEATHER AND SEASONS

بْآب ادْخُل كَرْمَك، أُقْطُف عَنقودَك ولا تِسْتهاب

In August, enter your vineyard and pick your clusters without fear.

This is related to the grape season in Lebanon, when grape clusters ripen and are ready to pick. This means do not have fear and hesitate to pick them at this time of the year as the grapes have ripened by then. The proverb calls for taking the right action when the right time comes.

cf. Wait till the time is ripe.

بْآذار بْتِغْلا المُونة وبْيِكْتَرّ النَّقار

In March, food becomes expensive, and households become quarrelsome.

بأيلول ثموّن لَعْيالَك واخْلِ الهَم عن بالَك

In September, store [winter] provisions for your children, and give peace to your mind.

This saying portrays the village life in Lebanon. It refers to winter storage which starts in September – the month of harvesting. Villagers start collecting supplies, including food and fuel to be ready for a hard winter. In September, the peasant can sell his grapes, figs, and all his harvest in order to buy what he needs for winter. In winter, the shops in the mountains are closed because of the severe cold. They say if you enter a villager's house in winter, you will find all sorts of grains, including wheat, chick peas, and lentil, dried meat, olives, olive oil, wine, pickles, jam in generous quantities, as well as firewood for chimneys.

Hence, the saying means that the peasant who has a big family or many mouths to feed cannot put his mind in rest, unless he collects winter storage that would last his family for long months to come.

cf. Save for a rainy day/ Always put something by for a rainy day.

بْأَيلول دَبِّر المَكْيول للعَدَس والحُمُّص والْفول

In September have your measure ready for lentils, chick-peas and beans.

These are the basic grains a Lebanese farmer would store for the cold winter season.

بْعِيد السَّيْدِة صُفُّوا العِنَب عَ المايْدِة

After Lady Day [Mary, 15th August] arrange the grapes on the table.

At this time of the year in Lebanon, grapes are ripe and tasty, and one can offer them to visitors.

شْحَالْة التِّين في التَّشارين

The time for pruning fig trees is in October and November.

طَبَّاخ العِنَب والتِّين

The cooker of grapes and figs.

This refers to fog in early summer. It is believed that such humidity speeds up the ripening of grapes and figs in Lebanon, as if the humidity cooks them.

في تِشرين وَدِّع العِنب والتِّين

In October bid grapes and figs farewell.

كِل أَرض وإلها بْذار

Each kind of soil has its seeds.

Meaning every land is suitable for a specific plant.

كِلّ الأَشْجار بْتِتْعرَّى بْكانون ما عَدا العَفْص والصَّنْوْبَر والزَّيتون

In December and January all trees shed their leaves except for oak, pine, and olive.

This is said of trees found in Lebanon.

لَوْ بَدّها تشَنِّي كَعك كانت غَيِّمت عَجين

If it were going to rain cakes, the sky would have clouded with dough.

Meaning I should have seen that coming, or there are always signs by which we are able to tell something is going to happen.

مِتْل الخيار، أَوَّلتُه لِلْكِبار وآخِرتُه لِلْحمار

Like cucumbers, the first are for the rich, but later [ones] are for the donkey.

In the old days cucumbers could only be obtained during their harvesting season. When first harvested, they were dear and served only to the rich. But by the end of the cucumber season, when people had had enough of them, they ended up throwing them to the animals as fodder. This is said of unworthy people or of things that are of bad quality for they cannot have a lasting value.

GOOD AND BAD LUCK

بَعدْ ما وِصْلِت اللَّقمة لِلتَّم

After the mouthful had reached the mouth [it fell out].

Said when things can go wrong at the very last minute.

بْيِركُض بْيِركُض والعَشا خِبَّيزة

He runs and runs but supper is mallow.

Said of a person who works hard but doesn't get much return for it.

بْيِركُض وَرَا الرّغِيف والرّغِيف بْيرْكُض قِدَّامُه

He runs after the loaf, but the loaf runs away from him.

A similar proverb referring to someone who works hard, but cannot earn or attain what he deserves.

بْيَعْطي الجَوْز لِلّ ما عِنْدُه سْنان

[God] grants walnuts to those who have no teeth.

This is said enviously of people who get good chances in life but don't know how to use or benefit from them.

It is also said of people who are bestowed with wealth and abundance, but can't enjoy life either because of old age or bad health.

صَام سِنِة وْفَطَر على بَصَلِة

He fasted for a whole year, then broke his fast on an onion.

During the month of Ramadan, people have very big meals to break their fast. This proverb is said of those who wait for something patiently and then do not get eventually what they actually deserve.

عَ حِجّة الوَرْد يِشرَب العِلِّيْق

Because of the roses, the wild blackberry is watered.

As we water roses, we also happen to water wild plants, like blackberry shrubs. The proverb is said of those who do what is good without distinguishing between those who deserve it and those who don't. Like the sun that shines on everyone, so can you plant goodness everywhere, as it will never go to waste. This proverb is also said when we receive charity because of our relationship with someone more fortunate than ourselves.

قَليل الحَظ بيلاقِي العَظْم في الكِرْشة

The unlucky man finds a bone in the tripe.

Some people eat the tripe of an animal. It is unlikely that we would find a bone in tripe. This is said of unlucky people.

قَمْحَة وَلا شعيرَة؟

Wheat or barley?

Positive (wheat) or negative (barley)?

This is because people prefer wheat to barley. Wheat is commonly seen as the source of human food, a symbol of fertility and abundance, whereas, barley used to be seen as livestock fodder. This also has a story that dates back to Ancient Egypt. Pregnant women used to figure out how to determine the gender of a baby by urinating on wheat and barley seeds. If the barley sprouted, then the woman was carrying a boy, and if the wheat sprouted, she was carrying a girl. This question became a tradition: Wheat or barley?

كَب القَهوة خَير

Spilling coffee is a good omen.

Said to show that even bad luck or a very bad situation must have some good results.

cf. It's an ill wind that blows nobody any good.

ENTERTAINING AND HOSPITALITY

الأكل عَ قدّ المَحبّة

One's eating shows one's love.

This is said to the hostess or said by a generous hostess to her guests. This means if you eat much, you love your host or hostess very much.

أكلِة وإنْسَمِت عَلَيْك، كُول وبَحْلِق عَيْنَيْك

This is a meal that was cooked for you, so eat with your eyes wide open.

This is said jokingly to someone who may be shy when receiving hospitality. It is an invitation to feel at home and eat as much as you like.

بَيْت السَّبْع ما بِيخْلى من العْظام

The lion's den is never devoid of bones.

When someone who is asked to donate, or give or lend and tries to deny that he has anything to give, the one asking would quote this saying.

بْيِلهي الحُمار عَنْ عَليقُه

He distracts a donkey from eating his fodder.

Said jokingly of a good entertainer, or disapprovingly of someone who chatters.

الجُود مِن المَوْجود

Be generous with what is available.

This is said when we have limited ingredients for our visitors; however, we manage to do well. This is also said when we can only be generous or do well with what is available, for we can only be generous with what we have.

الحلُو مِن حَلاوتِها، والملح مِن عَجاقتُها

Saltlessness is because of her sweetness, saltiness is because of her untidiness.

A flattering remark for a woman who apologizes for lack of salt in her food.

غِنى بَلا سَخا مِثْل شجَرة بَلا تَمَر

To be rich without being generous is like a tree without fruit.

الفَضْلِة لِلْفَضيل

The remaining food is for the virtuous.

This is said as an excuse to offer the last bit of food to a guest. The play on words (alliteration) makes it effective in Arabic.

اللّقمة الّي بتمُّه مِش إلُه

The mouthful in his mouth is not his.

Literally speaking, this person might deprive himself of his own meal to give it to the needy. It is said of a generous and noble person who sacrifices everything he has for the sake of his family or those in need, even if this person does not have much to give.

cf. He/she has a heart of gold/ He'd give his last penny to a beggar.

لاقيني ولا تُعَشِّيني

Welcome me rather than just offer me dinner.

An admonition to be welcoming, as what your guest expects from you is a smiling face rather than just offering him food or drink with a grumpy face.

DESTINY

الحَبِّة (حبّة القَمح) بِتْحور وْبِتدور وبتنزَل تَحت الكور (وبترْجَع لِلكور)
A grain [of wheat] goes round and round; finally it goes through the funnel.
Said of something which completes its journey to a special end.

اشتَهيْنا الدَّجاجِة أَكلْناها بْريشها
We craved a chicken; we ate it with its feathers.
This is said when people long for something, but when they get hold of the opportunity, they fail to deal with it successfully. Another meaning, is that when one longs for something, it is very probable that something might go wrong, which spoils one's enjoyment.

رِجْعِت المَيّ لمجَاريها
The water has gone back to its usual course.
Things have gone back to normal.

LOVE AND MARRIAGE

أكَلْني بِعْيونه

He was eating me with his eyes.

This is said when a beautiful girl is conscious of a man staring at her; or when someone stares at you.

خَبِّ العَسل بِجْرارُه تَتجي أسْعارُه

Hide the honey in its jars until [good] prices come.

One should keep the valuable things, till the right time comes in order to sell them with profit. Although this proverb is used for materialistic things on the market, it is also said to single women, metaphorically, when they decide to marry in haste. In the Middle East, women are considered very precious to their own families. Hence, this proverb is advice to avoid marrying a man who is likely to make her poor or unhappy.

cf. Marry in haste, repent at leisure.

خِبْز وبَصَلة بِرْياحة، ولا خَروف مِحْشي بِصْياحها

Bread and onion with peace, is better than a stuffed lamb with her yelling.

The best thing in life is peace of mind even if one has to live a simple life. But if a man lives a tense life surrounded by an atmosphere of divisions and differences with his wife for instance, even the best food with her will not taste good. This signifies the importance of peace of mind and contentment.

زَوَان بَلدك وْلا قَمْح الصَّليبي

The darnel of your own homeland is better than the wheat of the crusader.

Darnel is a weed that is usually cleared from the wheat fields. This expression means rather marry a homely woman from your homeland than marry a beautiful stranger.

زَيْتاتنا عَ سْلاطاتنا

Our own oil on our own salad.

This is a similar proverb meaning do not marry out of the community. This is taken from village life in the Levant where people take pride in consuming their own olive oil.

شو أنا جارية بِتقشّر بَصل بِمَطبَخَك؟

Do you think I am a slave who peels onions in your kitchen?

An expression said by a woman who is mistreated by her husband.

ضَرْب الحَبيبْ زْبيب، وِحْجارْتُه رُمَّان

The beloved's blows are like raisins, and his stoning is like pomegranates.

Said to someone you love even if she or he hurts you.

على قَلْبي أَحْلى من العَسَل

It feels sweeter than honey to my heart.

This is usually said when someone asks you for a favour and you assure this person that you will do it for him or her with pleasure, out of love, and care, and without expecting anything in return.

cf. Your wish is my command.

كِل فُولِة مْسَوَّسة إِلْها كَيَّال أَعْوَر

Each wormy horse bean gets its one-eyed weigher.

Said of marriage, meaning that even an unattractive-looking girl will find her man.

LIARS AND CHEATS

بْياكُلْ راس الحَيِّة

He eats the head of a snake.

Said of someone who is a big cheat.

دَخَّانَك عِمانا وْطَعام ما جَانا

Your smoke has blinded us, but no food has come to us.

This is said of someone who gives words without action. This is similar to a man who fools people by telling them he has food cooking just by starting fire, but no food comes.

خِبْزْنا أَبيض مِن خِبْزكُم. قال له: كَذِّبْني بِرغيف

"Our bread is whiter than yours!" He said: "Prove it by giving me a loaf."

Don't brag, have something to prove.

HOPELESSNESS

حَمَّضِت

It has gone sour.
Said of something when it becomes stale or boring.

الدَّبُّور لا يُعطي عَسلاً

The wasp does not give honey.
This is said when something is impossible.
cf. You cannot get blood out of a stone.

دِقْ المَيّ مَيّ

Pound water and it remains water.
Meaning it is useless.

سَمك في بَحْر

A fish in a sea.
Said when searching for something extremely hard to find.
   cf. It's like finding a needle in a haystack.

لا قِدْرتَك تِغلي ولا مِقلايْتك تِقلي
وأنا مَرّيت عليك من قِلّة عَقلي

Nothing boils in your pot and nothing fries in your pan; but I dropped by out of my stupid mind.
   Said to useless people or when you waste your time on useless people.

مِلْحة وذابت

A pinch of salt that dissolved.

It is very commonly said when something disappears without any trace, so better to forget about it.

LAZINESS

أَكَلْها على بارد المِسْتَريح

He ate it in a cool restful way.

Said of someone who gets something with a great deal of ease without having exerted any effort.

سِت وجارتَين عَ قَلي بَيْضْتَين

A housewife with two neighbours [just] to fry two eggs.

Said sarcastically of a team wasting time and making a fuss over nothing.

قَالوا لها قُومي طبُخي، قَالت مَريضَة
قالوا لها قومي كِلي، قالت وين ملعقتي العَريضة

They told her: Get up and cook; she said: I'm sick.

They told her: Get up and eat; she said: Where is my big spoon?

Said of lazy and selfish people, who can't even do you a small favour.

الكَسل ما بْيِطْعَم عسَل

Laziness does not feed you honey.
Sitting around won't get anything done.

مِثْل خَيْل الدَّولة، أَكْل وْمَرعى وقِلّة صَنْعَة

Like the horses of the State: they eat, graze and do nothing.

The basis of this proverb dates back to when the Lebanese government used to own horses to be used for specific missions; but those missions were rare. Thus, during the remaining days of the year such horses barely did any job, they were loose in the fields grazing, or eating hay in the stables. This proverb applies to people of undeserved wealth. Such people do not work hard for a living, or earn an income from a particular source without doing a job to deserve it. An equivalent phrase in English is *it's a sinecure*.

cf. The fat cats.

SPENDTHRIFTS AND SAVERS

إلّي عنده بْهار بِرُشّ ع الخِبَّيْزة /التِلّيع

He who has pepper [let him] sprinkle it on mallow.

Pepper or spices in the old days were not easy to get and were expensive, and therefore only used with certain delicacies. So to sprinkle spices on mallow or cheap foods was considered very extravagant. Pepper is metaphorical for money. It is said to spendthrift people who have a lot of money and can spend it on frivolous things.

كوُل سنة بَصل واِضْمن لْنَفسَك باقي السّنين عَسَل

Eat onions for one year, after which you can guarantee that your food will be honey.

Advice to save money.

PRETENSIONS AND SNOBBERY

إذا كَثُرت الألوان (ألوان الصّحون) اعرف أنّها من بيوت الجيران

If the colours [of plates] vary, you know that they come from the neighbours' houses.

In the village, some boastful people borrow things from their neighbours in order to entertain their guests. This is said of pretentious people who usually borrow to boast or impress others.

أكَل فولُه وْرِجِع لأُصُوله

He ate horse beans and returned to his origins.

Said when people show symptoms that they originally belonged to the lower classes, despite their apparent wealth and luxury.

بيَعمل الدّنيا بَيضة وبيقَشّرْها

He makes the world [look like] an egg and then peels it.

This mockingly refers to a person who fabricates stories and makes them sound true. It is also said of someone who thinks he can easily do anything in this world.

دَخَلْنا دارْكم وْشِفْنا فْشارْكُم، وْعَرَفْنا عَشانا مِنْ عَشا حُمارْكم

We have been to your house; we have seen your vanity; now we know what you have for supper [after seeing] your donkey's supper

Said of vain people who conceal their poverty, yet pretend in front of others they live luxuriously. The proverb says mockingly there is not much difference between what those people have for supper and what their donkey has.

دُسوتُهم عالِية وبُطونُهم خَالِية

Their cooking pots are high, but their stomachs are empty.

When there is costly furniture in a house, but no provision, nor money. A similar proverb mocking pretentious and vain people.

الطَّويل بْياكُل تِين، والقَصير بِموت حَزين

He who is tall eats figs; he who is short dies sadly.

This shows preference for a tall stature. The proverb is influenced by life in the village where only the tall can reach up to get figs from a fig tree.

الفلّاح فلّاح وْلَوْ أَكل الشَّوْرَبا بالشَّوْكِة

A farmer is a farmer even if he eats his soup with a fork.

The farmer might imitate civilized folks who use knife and fork when eating. In doing so, he does silly things. This means no matter what the farmer does to look more modern, he remains a simple farmer.

كُول عَ ذَوْقَك والبُس عَ ذَوْق النَّاس

Eat to your taste, but wear clothes to the taste of others.

One's appearance must be in line with the social conventions and people do judge you first by what you wear.

لا البَطّيخ بْيِكْسِر سيخ، وْلا المَلفوف بْيِلْوي سْيوف

Neither a watermelon can break knives, nor can a cabbage bend swords.

A pretentious person cannot harm you.

ما في حَلاوِة غَيْر بِبْعَلبك؟

Is there no halva except in Baalbek?

Said to a man who claims that he has got the best and no one else but him. Baalbek is a Roman city in Lebanon.

مغَطّى بِقِشرة بَصلة

Covered with an onion skin.

Said of someone concealing his poverty or unworthiness.

WATER

مِثِل السَّمَك، إن طِلِعْ بَرَّاتِ المَي بِموت
Like fish who die out of water.

Said of people who like swimming or living near the sea.

RESPECT AND DISRESPECT

مِش كِلّ اللَّحوم بْتِتَّاكل

Not all flesh is edible.

To eat someone's flesh is to mistreat him. This is said when some people force you to respect them when you attempt to mistreat them because they are more powerful, more respectable, or more righteous.

مِنْ عِمِل حالُه نْخالِة بَحْوَشوه الدَجاج

He who makes of himself bran, chickens shall scratch into it.

This is said of people who don't impose their own self-respect or who lower themselves by misconduct; therefore, they will naturally be mistreated and degraded by others.

USEFULNESS AND HANDINESS

الزَّيت عِماد البيت

[Olive] oil is the pillar of our home.

Shows the importance of olive oil and its different uses to people living in the Levant.

كِلُّه مَنافِع مِثل زَيْت الغَار

He is like laurel oil, full of uses.

Laurel, *known as bay or bay laurel in the UK,* is a plant used for medication and for seasoning in cooking. Its extracted oil is used as aroma in the soap industry.

This can be said about a handy, versatile person.

cf. He's a Jack-of-all-trades.

THE MARKET

إذا ارتَفَع سِعر الشّعير، بيرخص سِعر الحَمِير

If the price of barley goes higher, the price of donkeys goes lower.

When there is inflation, material things become more valuable than the living.

عالسّكين يا بَطّيخ

A watermelon [cut] with a knife.

This is street vendors' calls to sell watermelons. A watermelon vendor would convince customers to buy his watermelons by showing his willingness to cut the watermelon with a knife, to show its good colour and quality, as the condition of the inside is unpredictable. If the buyer took it home without knowing its condition, he would regret not buying it "cut with a knife". This is advice to study things well in advance or take safe measures before embarking on a project that could end up in failure.

EMBARRASMENT AND REGRET

أكل أصابِعُه نَدامة

He ate his fingers out of regret.

Someone who is full of regret.

مِثل خِبزِ الوَقْف، فَرَح بِالتِّم عَزا بِالْبَطْن

Like bread of the waqf: happiness in the mouth, but a funeral in the stomach.

Waqf bread is alms bread given free by the church for poor people. Said when someone is glad to get a free loaf of bread, but the free bread is of bad quality. This refers to things that taste good but are harmful.

مِثل صُبَّيرة طَمْسُن

Like Thomson's cactus-fig.

This is a kind of cactus which grows on the coast of Lebanon and gives a tasty fruit. They say an English doctor in Beirut was offered cactus-figs to eat. As it was the first time he saw this fruit, he tried to take out the seeds. However, he soon discovered that the whole fig was a collection of seeds. This is said in situations when you are introduced to something exotic for the first time and handled it foolishly.

بَلَع بْرِيقُه

He swallowed his saliva.

Said of someone who is embarrassed or put in a difficult position from which escape is difficult.

بَلَع لسانُه

He swallowed his tongue.
He can't speak anymore because he is shocked.

يا بيّاع الزَّيْت شو مَعَك؟

You who sell olive-oil, what have you got [to sell]?
Said mockingly when you hear a stupid question.

يا مِستَّرخِص اللّحم، عِند المَرَق تِنْدَم

You, who buy cheap meat, when you come to the broth you will regret it.

This proverb asks one not to choose cheap things to save money, because the result will be disappointing. This analogy is related to many fields in life. If we choose cheap tools or labour, then we won't get good results.

THE DRUNKARDS

بْيِسْكَر مِنْ زْبِيبِة

He gets drunk from a single raisin.
This mocks people who get drunk easily.

بْيِشرَب من الجَزْمِة

He drinks from the shoe.
Said of drunken people who drink to extremes. They would drink even if the alcohol came from a shoe!

HEALTH

الأَكِل بيجِرّ الأَكِل

Eating drags eating.

One's appetite grows whenever a person starts eating. This is advice for people not to overeat. It is also said to greedy, corrupt people who don't know their limits.

الأَكل نِصْفه يُقيت ونِصْفه يُميت

Half of what we eat makes us live and the other half kills.

Advice to avoid overeating and to eat food of good quality.

إتْعِب جِسْمَك وْلا تِتْعِب عَقْلَك

Tire out your body, but tire not your mind.

Physical exhaustion is more bearable than worrying.

إلّي كْثير جوعان ما بْياكُل منيح

He who is very hungry does not eat well.

When people are very hungry, they tend to eat very quickly and end up with indigestion.

إلِّي ما بْتِغْلي قِدْرْتُه ما بْتِشبَع زُكْرْتُه

If anyone's pot boils not, his belly button will not be satisfied.

Belly button refers to the stomach. This means only proper cooking satisfies hungry stomachs. Cold foods do not satisfy.

امشِ بِدائك ما مشَى بِك

Keep walking in your sickness as long as you can.

An Islamic proverb meaning as long as sickness does not become serious, keep up your activities; for illness increases when you worry more about it. Feeling positive can dispel sickness and boost immunity.

cf. Try to walk it off.

أوَّل العِنب وآخِر التِّين

The first of the grapes and the last of the figs.

In the Levant, people wait for the beginning of summer to eat ripe grapes. By the end of summer, figs become ripe and tasty. This is said about eating fruit in their own season to enjoy their good taste and to benefit from their healthy qualities.

بَطْن مَلان كَيْف تَمام

Satisfied stomach, good mood.

بَطْن الاِنسان عدُوَّه

Man's stomach is his own enemy.

Overeating, or eating food which is fatty or of bad quality, is harmful to one's health.

البَلَد اللّي بْتَصَلْها كُلْ مِن بَصَلْها

Eat the onions of the [new] country you reach.

Advice for travelers who should eat onions to stay healthy and strong, as there is a common belief that onions make one immune against colds or stomach aches.

تْغَدَّ وِتْمَدَّ، تْعَشَّ وِتْمَشَّ

After lunch, take a siesta; after supper, take a stroll.

A Middle-Eastern habit which calls for rest after lunch and a walk after supper to stay healthy.

تفَاحة كُلّ يَوم تُبْعد الطَّبيب إلى الأبَد

An apple a day keeps the doctor away.

تِمَّك إلَك، بَطْنك مِش إلَك

Your mouth is yours, your stomach is not yours.

Advice to avoid overeating because eventually no-one can control stomach pain or illness.

cf. Your eyes are bigger than your belly.

التِّين مسامير الرّكَب

Figs are the nails of the knees.
Eating figs is believed to make one very strong.

الثُّوم قَتَّال السّموم

Garlic is an antidote.

الثُّوم مَأكول مَذْموم ، وَلو شفى كلّ السّموم

Garlic is an offensive food, even if it remedies all diseases.

الجَزَر يُقَوِّي النَّظَر

Carrots strengthen one's eyesight.
cf. Carrots will make you see in the dark.

الخِبْز الحاف بيعَرِّض الكْتاف

Plain bread makes one's shoulders broad.
Eating plain bread makes you sturdy.

دِرْهَم وقاية أَحْسن مِن قِنْطار عِلاج

A gram of prevention is better than a ton of medicine.

It is better to try to avoid health problems in the first place, rather than trying to fix them with expensive remedies.

cf. Prevention is better than cure.

شَبْعان مِن حَليب إمُّه

Well-fed from his mother's milk.

A very strong person.

طَعام الأَسَد تُخْمة للذِّيب

The food of the lion is gluttony for the wolf.

Advice against overeating. Also means that those who are not used to having wealth do not know how to handle it.

cf. Gluttony kills more than the sword.

عصَافير بَطنُه تُزَقْزِق

The birds of his stomach are tweeting.

He is very hungry.

عِندما تَتناوَل لَذيذ الغِذاء تَذَكَّر مَرارَة الدَّواء

When you eat tasty food, remember the bitter taste of medicine.

Advice given to those who overeat or don't watch their diet.

العَين جِيعانِة والمِعْدِة شَبْعانِة

The eye is hungry, but the stomach is well-satisfied.

cf. His eyes are bigger than his stomach.

Also said of corrupt politicians or a greedy person who is very wealthy but is always asking for more.

فاكِهَة الدِّيار بِتطوّل الأَعْمار

Home fruits bring longevity.

It is healthier to grow and eat our own fruit and organic vegetables which grow in their own season and from our own fields.

فَرَح في التَّم عَزا في البَطن

Joy in the mouth; a funeral in the stomach.

Said of delicacies which are tasty but harmful to the stomach.

قلِّل طَعامَك تحمد مَنامك، قلِّل كَلامك تَحْفظ مَقامَك

Eat less and sleep well, talk less and sit tall.

Overeating ends in indigestion that can deprive you of a good sleep. Similarly, gossiping ends with loss of respect and social problems.

قَليل مِن السَّم نافِع، كثير من السُّكَّر مُضِرّ

A little poison is beneficial; much sugar is harmful.

Some toxic substances build a resistance in the body, but sugar-rich food is harmful to one's health.

كِلّ يَوْم عافِية بْيِسوى مُلْكِ الأَرْض

Each day of good health is worth all the wealth of the earth.

كَمْ مِنْ أَكلَةٍ مَنعَتْ أَكلاتٍ

Many a single eating prevents several eatings.

Literally said of a man who eats voraciously that he has to give up other meals because of gluttony. This is a religious proverb meaning indulging in vices ends in loss, defeat, disgrace or regret.

كُول أَوَّل الـعِنب وتْفَرَّج على خُدودَك، وكُول أَوَّل التِّين وتْفَرَّج على زْنُودَك

Eat the first harvest of grapes and watch your cheeks, eat the first harvest of figs and watch your arms.

Grapes are good for your blood and figs are good for your strength. The rhyming in Arabic matches with this traditional belief.

كُول البَصْلة صَباحاً وَحْدَك، وفي الظّهر شارِك فيها، وفي المَساء اترُكها لعَدُوَّك

Eat the onion in the morning alone, at noon share it, and in the evening leave it to your enemy.

This is a dietary advice for one to be moderate when eating onions, as people in the Middle East use onions in their diet almost on a daily basis. The advice is also social because some people offend others by the smell of their breath if they eat onions at the wrong time.

كُول دِبْس وزَيْت وناطِح الحَيط

Eat molasses and olive oil and butt against a wall.

Molasses (from grapes) and oil provide you with unusual strength that makes you as strong as a bull.

كُول قَليل بتْعيش كثير

Eat little, live long.

كُول مِن كل شي ولا تكَثِّر مِن شي

Eat from everything, but with small quantities.
Be moderate.

مِثْل شِرْب الدَخَّان، لا أَوَّلُه بِسْمِ الله، ولا آخْرُه الحَمدِ لله

Like smoking, it does not begin 'In the name of God', nor does it end 'Thanks be to God.'

A pious Muslim would say "In the name of God," before starting to eat or drink, and "Thanks be to God," after finishing. However, this cannot be applied to smoking.

ناسْ بتاكُل لَتْعيش، وْناسْ بِتْعيش لَتاكُل

Some people eat in order to live, and some people live in order to eat.

Advice to eat in moderation.
cf. Eat to live, don't live to eat.

نام بَكِّير وْقُوم بَكِّير وْشوف الصّحَة كيف بِتْصير

Sleep early, rise early, and see how your health will be.

cf. Early to bed and early to rise, makes a man healthy, and wealthy, and wise.

نَحْن قَومٌ لا نَأْكُل حَتَّى نَجُوع وإذا أَكَلْنا لا نَشْبَع

We are people who do not eat till we get hungry, and once we eat we don't get full.

An Islamic proverb which gives advice on how to live healthily.

نَوْمِة عَ بُكْرَة بِتْرَبِّي الشَّحْم عَ الزُّكْرَة

To sleep late in the morning grows fat on one's belly.

يَأكُل مِن راس شْفافُه

He eats through the tips of his lips.

This is said of someone who eats with disgust or without appetite.

REFERENCES

Al-Musawi, A. (1971) *Nahju Al Balagha (English Translation from Arabic).* Iran: Ansariyan Publications

Al-Rasi, S. (1995) *Kal AlMathal.* Beirut: Nawfal

Arnander P. & Skipwith, A. (1988) *The Son of a Duck is a Floater.* London: Stacey International

Freyha, A. (1974) *A Dictionary of Modern Lebanese Proverbs.* Beirut: Librairie Du Liban

Khahwaji, S. (2005) *Faraed AlAmthal Allubnanieh.* Beirut: Dar AlMalaffat

Kiwan, A. (2008) *Kamous Alamthal (English-Arabic).* Beirut: Daralhilal

Ridout, R. & Witting C. (1969) *English Proverbs Explained.* London: Pan Books

http://www.phrases.org.uk › Phrase Dictionary - Meanings and Origins